IMAGES
of America

GREAT LAKES
NAVAL TRAINING STATION

EARLY VIEW. This view, taken while the base was under construction, overlooks what would become the main parade field in front of the administration building. "Brick Row," the senior officer housing, can be seen in the distance.

On the cover: **ROSS FIELD, C. 1935.** Pictured is a seabag inspection by Rear Adm. John Downes. (Courtesy of the Great Lakes Naval Museum.)

IMAGES
of America

GREAT LAKES
NAVAL TRAINING STATION

Therese Gonzalez

ARCADIA
PUBLISHING

Published by Arcadia Publishing
Charleston SC, Chicago IL, Portsmouth NH, San Francisco CA

Printed in the United States of America

Library of Congress Catalog Card Number: 2007938999

For all general information contact Arcadia Publishing at:
Telephone 843-853-2070
Fax 843-853-0044
E-mail sales@arcadiapublishing.com
For customer service and orders:
Toll-Free 1-888-313-2665

Visit us on the Internet at www.arcadiapublishing.com

This book is dedicated to all the sailors who trained at Great Lakes.

CONTENTS

ACKNOWLEDGMENTS

Naval Station, Great Lakes, home of the navy's Recruit Training Command, as well as many other technical training schools, is a very special place. When it opened in 1911, I am sure the founders had no idea that their quiet little base would play such an important role in history and later become the home of the U.S. Navy's only boot camp.

Much of the wonderful history would not fit in this book, but preservation continues and future plans include a new museum to tell the history of the enlisted sailors who crossed the quarterdeck of the navy at Great Lakes.

Many historians and friends of Great Lakes helped in the preparation of this book, including members of the Great Lakes Naval Museum Association, the Naval Service Training Command and Navy Region Midwest public affairs offices, Beverly Dawson of the Glenview Historical Society, Eric Lundahl and Bill Christensen of the Hangar One Foundation, and the many sailors who have donated their artifacts and memories. Special thanks go to the first museum curators, Leland "Trig" and Dottie Watson, for their wonderful organization and meticulous files. Unless otherwise indicated, the photographs are courtesy of the archives of the Great Lakes Naval Museum.

I would like to thank Arcadia editor Jeff Ruetsche for recognizing that this book needed to be written and allowing me the extra time I needed to write it. Finally I would like to thank my wonderful family who give me strength and love.

INTRODUCTION

On a February night, a U.S. battleship was anchored in a foreign port. The ship was sent to "show the flag," to demonstrate the United States' presence in a region of the world with rising tensions. The crew was warned to remain on alert and withstanders were vigilant. Despite their best efforts, at 9:40 p.m., a massive explosion tore the ship apart, ending the lives of over 250 American sailors. The blackened ship sank to the bottom of the harbor.

This was not the USS *Cole* in 2000 in the Port of Yemen; it was the USS *Maine* in Havana Harbor, Cuba, in 1898. The USS *Maine* explosion led to the United States' war against Spain and sparked a remarkable growth of the U.S. Navy, and the establishment of the United States Naval Training Station, Great Lakes, Illinois.

During the late 1800s, the U.S. Navy had been trying to provide American warships with intelligent, trained, and professional crews. The officer corps was not the problem. The difficulty was the enlisted men. Life onboard any ship of the 1700s and 1800s was a tough, hard life and not one that many men wanted. During wartime, sailors were kidnapped from docks and harbors and shanghaied into service aboard foreign ships. Many sailors who were serving willingly were not exactly model citizens. They were, for the most part, foreign, indigent laborers who traveled the world, moving from warship to merchant ship and back again. Crews were made up of professional sailors but not professional U.S. Navy men. On some ships, few besides the officers spoke English and were U.S. citizens. There was no guarantee that the crew would be loyal to the United States. Changes in recruitment and training were aimed to fix this.

During the Spanish-American War, the U.S. Navy realized that over half of the men joining the navy were coming from the Midwest. Before this, it had focused recruiting and training efforts on the Atlantic and Pacific coasts, because where there was salt water, there were ships and sailors looking for work. Nevertheless, the Midwest was a surprisingly rich source of ambitious young men, looking for training and life out of the cornfields. Experience could be gained and skills could be taught to these willing volunteers.

Illinois congressman George E. Foss, who was serving as the chairman of the House Committee on Naval Affairs, suggested that a naval base in the Midwest would be advisable to train these volunteers closer to home rather than sending them all the way to the coast.

Several locations were examined and extensive debates were argued, but eventually a site at Lake Bluff, Illinois, was selected, in great part through the efforts of businessman Graeme Stewart.

CONGRESSMAN FOSS. George E. Foss saw an opportunity and seized it. Foss was the station's "man in Washington."

GRAEME STEWART. A prominent political figure and member of the prestigious Merchants Club of Chicago, Graeme Stewart worked ceaselessly until funds were available to buy 172 acres of land on Lake Michigan. The cost of this land to the U.S. government was $1; the cost to Stewart was his life. He suffered a fatal stroke in May 1905, just after the land was transferred.

One

CONSTRUCTION

Once the Lake Bluff site was under naval control, Capt. Albert Ross, U.S. Navy, was assigned as the first commandant of the naval station. Captain Ross, while an experienced instructor in the navy's apprentice program and at the U.S. Naval Academy as well as in a variety of other training duties, was not an experienced base commander and knew little of architecture and engineering. However, Secretary of the Navy Paul Morton brushed aside Captain Ross's comment that he was "just a plain sailorman and [knew] nothing about land construction work."

A short time later, Captain Ross and civil engineer George A. McKay, U.S. Navy, reported to Great Lakes and went to work. Between 1905 and 1911, they met often with Jarvis Hunt, a prominent Chicago architect who was selected to design the layout of the base and architecture of the buildings.

The Lake Bluff site had been carefully chosen and was a beautiful piece of land. Right on Lake Michigan, with a natural harbor, it was crisscrossed by Pettibone Creek, which emptied into the lake. Jarvis Hunt took advantage of this natural division and designed a layout that allowed for different functions on the four natural plateaus created by the creek.

The base was planned to train 1,500 men at any given time with provision for additional buildings should the need arise. Hunt designed a beautiful base, functional yet harmonious with red brick, terra-cotta ornamentation, and designs to create a unifying nautical theme.

The four plateaus were used for (1) the main training camp, (2) the receiving and isolation camp, (3) the naval hospital and (4) for the marine barracks and guardhouse.

"BRICK ROW." Seen here are the original senior officers' quarters at Great Lakes. These homes are still in use by the admirals and captains at Great Lakes. The large home at the left of the

REAR ADM. ALBERT ROSS. Although on the retired rolls when the first company graduated, Albert Ross stayed until the first companies graduated. He was recalled to active duty in World War I.

picture has always been the base commander's house and occupied by the senior officer. The large flowered circle in front of it is known as Jarvis Hunt Circle.

JARVIS HUNT, BASE ARCHITECT. Jarvis Hunt's father and uncle were architects who had designed Newport, Rhode Island, "cottages" for the wealthy. Hunt hoped for similar grandeur at Great Lakes, but Rear Admiral Ross reminded him that taxpayers were footing the bill.

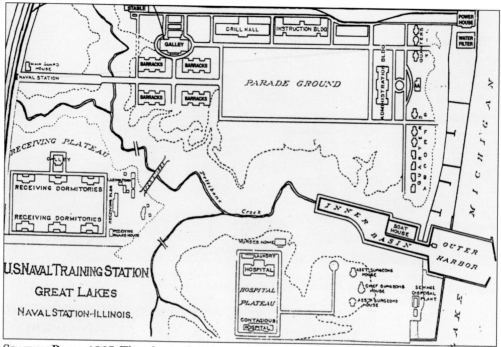

STATION PLAN, 1907. This plan included a stable northwest of the galley, and with the exception of a contagious hospital, this is the station as it was built.

BASE CONSTRUCTION. In this view, looking east toward Lake Michigan, the power plant smokestack can be seen in the distance.

Two

GREAT LAKES IS OPENED

Naval Training Station, Great Lakes was officially opened on July 1, 1911. While only a small staff was assigned, news coverage was extensive, and the details about the marvelous station included the massive drill hall, the state-of-the-art hospital, the large indoor swimming pool, and the centerpiece of the station—the administration building that was crowned by an imposing clock tower, visible from anywhere on the station.

On July 3, 1911, the first recruit arrived. Joseph Wallace Gregg was a slender 17-year-old from Terre Haute, Indiana. Returning for the 50th anniversary, he confessed, "I was a little shy, homesick, and didn't cut too much of a figure in my new Navy uniform."

According to the 1913 Naval Training Station, Great Lakes pamphlet,

> The recruits received at the Great Lakes Training Station come for the most part from the farms, villages and cities of the states of the great middle west. These young men are selected with the greatest care, and only those who conform to the Navy's high mental, physical and moral standard are accepted. Every applicant for enlistment is subjected to a rigorous physical examination, and a thorough inquiry is made into his character and antecedents. . . . The first consideration of the training station is to develop its apprentice seamen into men of character, self-reliance and usefulness, and it is astonishing to note the marked improvement effected in their make-up by the few months stay at the training station.

Gregg and his shipmates were assigned to Great Lakes for four months. On October 28, 1911, they graduated. Over 10,000 visitors came to watch them pass-in-review. On the reviewing platform were Pres. William H. Taft, Rear Adm. Albert Ross (who was on the retired list but allowed to stay to see the first company graduate), Secretary of the Navy George Von L. Meyer, and Congressman George E. Foss. President Taft dedicated the new station "to our country, our God, and our flag."

The Tower
by EDWARD D. GOURLEY
SEAMAN 2ND CLASS

THE old administration tower
With fitting dignity and power
Soars into clear or cloudy skies
With equal strength. Its walls arise,
A weatherbeaten mass of thick
Unyielding lime and brick.

AND near its airy wind-worn top
Is set the trusty station clock;
A most relentless piece of works
That has no time for Jackie shirks.
From early morn 'till colors fall
It keeps things straight for one and all.

THIS faithful clock, if it could say
Aught else besides the time of day,
Might paint a grand and thrilling sight
Of what it sees from such a height:
The drills, the hundred tent-lined lanes
The lake, the dipping hydroplanes.

BEFORE its front in full review
Have passed ten thousand boys in blue,
While Taft, T. R., Rear Admiral Ross,
Josephus Daniels, Edmund Foss,
Have watched the lines of marching feet
Keep time to martial music's beat.

THIS tower when storm clouds scurry by
Defies the elements on high.
We, too, must rest unchanging, fixed;
Led on by lofty aims unmixed
With sordid ends. Stand firm. We, too,
Must be secure and true.

FRONTISPIECE. This illustration and poem, from a 1918 issue of the *Great Lakes Recruit* magazine, were drawn and written by Seaman Second Class Edward Gourley. Seaman Gourley was assigned to the Aviation Department and was a gifted illustrator. He drew and painted dozens of technical illustrations for the aviation schools as well as regularly contributing to the station newspaper and magazine.

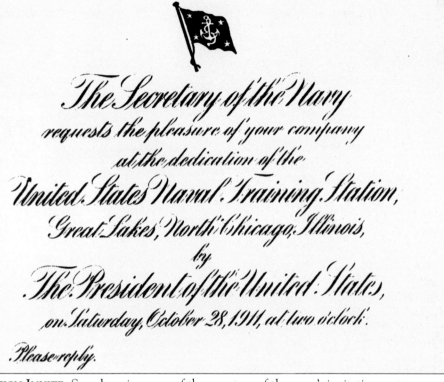

The Secretary of the Navy
requests the pleasure of your company
at the dedication of the
United States Naval Training Station,
Great Lakes, North Chicago, Illinois,
by
The President of the United States,
on Saturday, October 28, 1911, at two o'clock.
Please reply.

DEDICATION INVITE. Seen here is a copy of the secretary of the navy's invitation sent to guests attending the 1911 dedication of the station by the president of the United States. (Courtesy of Bob Battersby.)

HOSPITAL. Seen here is a 1914 view of the original naval training station hospital. At the time it was built, it was a state-of-the-art facility. Sunrooms for convalescing patients can be seen in the front of the building.

COMMISSIONING CEREMONY. Rear Adm. Albert Ross and his officers stand at attention in front of the administration building. A small crowd of spectators watches from the steps. This scene

took place on July 1, 1911.

Base Ball Team.

Band and Bugle Squad.
U.S. NAVAL TRAINING STATION, GREAT LAKES, ILLINOIS.

POSTCARD, 1914. Even in the early days of the station, sports and music were important. Competitive sports have long been used to build teamwork and strengthen sailors' bodies. The drum and bugle squad helped keep sailors in step during pass-in-review.

INSPECTION OF CLOTHING.
U.S. NAVAL TRAINING STATION GREAT LAKES, ILLINOIS.

INTERIOR VIEW OF RECRUIT BARRACKS, 1914. Recruits are shown during a seabag inspection of their clothing. A specific layout was taught to the recruits and was strictly judged by the inspecting officer.

JAMES SHELDON TRAYER. As a chief quartermaster, James Sheldon Trayer was the company commander of the first recruit company at Great Lakes. He later went on to a distinguished naval career, ultimately retiring as a lieutenant commander.

FIRST GRADUATING COMPANY AT GREAT LAKES. Chief Quartermaster James Sheldon Trayer stands in front. The first recruit to enter Great Lakes, Joseph Wallace Gregg is seated in front, second from the left.

THE ADMINISTRATION BUILDING, OCTOBER 1911. The building is decorated for the first recruit graduation ceremony. Draped flags are visible over the windows in front, directly behind the reviewing stand.

OFFICIAL PARTY ON THE REVIEWING STAND. In the forefront are Pres. William Howard Taft and Rear Adm. Albert Ross. Also shown are Secretary of the Navy George Von L. Meyer and Congressman George E. Foss.

Three

WORLD WAR I

By 1916, recruit training had expanded to include four special schools: radio/signal schools, the band school, and hospital corpsman school, and about 220 recruits were arriving per month. This changed in 1917 as the United States entered the war in Europe. In April 1917, when war was declared, the station received 9,027 recruits—300 per day. Great Lakes became the largest naval training station in the United States.

The original station included 39 brick buildings. By the time World War I ended in November 1918, Naval Training Station, Great Lakes had grown to 775 buildings supporting a population of 45,000. From declaration of war on April 6, 1917, to armistice on November 11, 1918, more than 125,000 men reported to Great Lakes for training. During this same period, 96,779 were sent to sea and 17,356 were graduated from special schools at the training station.

The rush of volunteers at first threatened to swamp the station. Cots placed under hammocks doubled the capacity of permanent barracks, and the drill hall and instruction buildings were used as barracks. Thousands of tents were procured and iron cots placed in each. The commandant, Capt. William Moffett, attempted to control the station's expansion, but facilities rapidly became inadequate.

Using the main station as a model regimental unit, Captain Moffett expanded the station by dividing it into self-contained regimental units. Each held 1,726 men and included an administration building, instruction building, drill hall, galley, barracks, dispensary, and heating plant. Construction of new wooden structures for 20,000 men began in July 1917. By October, seven were ready for occupancy, and men moved into double-floored, steam-heated barracks before winter.

The station Public Works Department was responsible for hiring construction firms to build the new barracks, but new barracks were needed faster than they could be built. A solution to this problem was found in new recruits with construction skills. These sailors drilled during the night and worked construction during the day. As their numbers increased, they became the 12th Regiment (Public Works). In one week during the summer of 1918, the 12th Regiment erected 35 temporary barracks in Camp Barry.

The first new school at Great Lakes trained new company commanders to train the flood of new recruits. Additional schools trained coxswains, quartermasters, gunners' mates, armed guards to man the merchant marine, artificers, aviation quartermasters, machinists' mates, armorers, ensigns for the Naval Reserve force, and aviation officers.

COMDR. WILLIAM ADGER MOFFETT. A brilliant leader, commander, and, later, admiral, William Adger Moffett went on to become the head of the Bureau of Naval Aviation.

AERIAL PHOTOGRAPH OF STATION EXPANSION, 1918. A camera attached to a kite and flown over the base took this photograph. It was first published in the *Great Lakes Recruit* magazine, and copies were later sold as souvenirs. Extensive construction is visible to the north (left side of the photograph) and to the west (right side of the photograph). The camps seen to the right of the railroad and Sheridan Road are the sites of today's Recruit Training Command.

JUST ARRIVED.

WORLD WAR I NEW RECRUITS. Still in their civilian clothes, these recruits wait in Camp Barry. New recruits were quarantined for three weeks in "incoming detention camps." Once certified healthy, they moved to the main training camps. The original isolation and receiving camp, Camp Barry was the first stop for all Great Lakes sailors until the early 1960s.

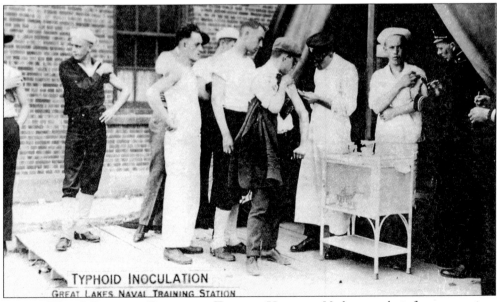

TYPHOID INOCULATION
GREAT LAKES NAVAL TRAINING STATION

WORLD WAR I RECRUITS RECEIVE A TYPHOID VACCINE. Unfortunately influenza vaccines were not available and hundreds of sailors at Great Lakes fell ill and many died during the Spanish influenza epidemic of 1917–1918.

SAILORS HEADING OUT TO WAR. The railroad had a spur extending onto the station, behind the galley and storehouse, out to the power plant. This photograph was taken behind Building Two, the general storehouse.

VIEW LOOKING SOUTH IN CAMP PERRY, WORLD WAR I. Immediately beyond is Building 602, the executive building for the 6th Regiment. The railroad track (see boxcar) divides the 5th and 6th Regiments. The barrel-roofed building in the rear is Drill Hall 600. Dispensary 605 with the curved driveway is immediately in front of the drill hall. To the extreme right is the YMCA Building 513. Just to the south is Contagious Ward 506, then Dispensary 505, and behind the railroad boxcar is the swimming school, Building 617. (Courtesy of the Illinois State Historical Library.)

LEARNING TO PACK DUFFLE © I.F.S. 191

SAILORS AND THEIR SEABAGS. Sailors still keep their belongings in duffel bags, or seabags. These World War I sailors at Camp Barry are learning to roll and stow all their belongings so that they all fit inside.

TEMPORARY BARRACKS UNDER CONSTRUCTION IN CAMP BARRY, JUNE 14, 1918. Sailors, led by the 12th Regiment "Fighting Tradesmen," built these barracks at fantastic rates. All the sailors were housed in these heated wooden barracks before winter. World War II construction battalions were modeled after the 12th Regiment, making Great Lakes the grandfather of

the U.S. Navy Seabees. Tradesmen initially spent three or four months at Great Lakes before transferring to sea duty or deploying to other commands. They became known as the "Fighting Tradesmen" because of their outstanding performance.

SEMAPHORE SIGNALS
GREAT LAKES NAVAL TRAINING STATION

SEMAPHORE SIGNALS. Signalmen passed orders of the day from the administration building around the base by semaphore. These sailors stand in front of the main flagpole, flanked by two Dahlgren guns.

1:15 P.M. BOAT DRILL FOR

©I.F.S. 1917

A "1:15 P.M. BOAT DRILL FOR AN HOUR." The 12-man crew is ready for practice.

STUDYING THE COMPASS
GREAT LAKES NAVAL TRAINING STATION

TEACHING NAVIGATION TO SAILORS. This entire platform was linked with tracks and pulleys so that as the ship's wheel turned, so did the platform.

STACKING RIFLES
GREAT LAKES NAVAL TRAINING STATION

RECRUITS STACKING 1903 SPRINGFIELDS. Recruits carried their rifles with them almost everywhere. When they were at ease or in training, they stacked their rifles. These recruits are by their tents on Ross Field, in front of the original drill hall.

ROPE SPLICING DRILL
GREAT LAKES NAVAL TRAINING STATION

ROPE-SPLICING DRILL. Recruits in World War I learned 37 different knots, hitches, and splices.

GAS ATTACK
GREAT LAKES NAVAL TRAINING STATION

GAS ATTACK TRAINING. World War I was the first war where soldiers, sailors, and marines were exposed to poisonous gas. Great Lakes sailors practice assaults wearing protective gear.

SPECIAL FORMATION OF SAILORS AT CAMP LOGAN. This camp was part of the U.S. Army's gun range at what is now Illinois State Beach Park. The anchor and target reflect the weapons training Great Lakes sailors learned at Camp Logan.

PAINTING OF WORLD WAR I YEOMAN (F). This painting is from the cover of a *Great Lakes Recruit* magazine. Women also trained and served at Great Lakes. Nineteen female yeomen or yeomen (F), "yeomenettes," provided clerical support for the Aviation and Public Works Departments. Yeomenettes at other bases worked in munitions plants, fingerprinting, intelligence, and communications.

Photo # 80-G-1037200 Josephine Beatrice Bowman

NAVY NURSE JOSEPHINE BEATRICE BOWMAN. Several U.S. Navy nurses as well as Lutheran Brotherhood nurses served onboard. The most famous was Josephine Beatrice Bowman, head of the Nursing Department at the station hospital and one of the "Sacred Twenty," the first 20 navy nurses. (Naval Historical Center photograph 80-G-1037200.)

SPECIAL FORMATION BY GREAT LAKES SAILORS. The main-side barracks can be seen at the top of the picture, Building Four off to the right. World War I gave Great Lakes Naval Training Station national recognition. A favorite throughout the war were the creative formations sailors made on patriotic or fund-raising occasions. Sometimes this took the form of a "living flag." In support of war bond sales, the sailors here form up to spell out *liberty* with white uniforms forming the letters against green grass.

**CELEBRATING THE 100,000TH RECRUIT AT
GREAT LAKES.** Before World War I, the station
trained 1,500 men at any given time. During
World War I, 126,000 were trained.

"A LIVING FLAG"
Covering seven acres composed of ten thousand Blue Jackets under command of
Captain W. A. Moffett, Commandant, at the World's greatest Naval Training Station,
Great Lakes, Illinois, November, 1917.

THE LIVING FLAG. This formation is made
up of 10,000 Great Lakes sailors and officers.
The original photograph was published
in the *Great Lakes Recruit* magazine, and
copies were sold to raise money for the Navy
Relief Society, a charitable organization for
sailors. This photograph by Arthur Mole
was one of several he photographed around
the country at various military bases. Other
subjects included the Statue of Liberty, a
bust of Pres. Woodrow Wilson, the Liberty
Bell, and an American eagle with its
wings outstretched.

33

MAIN GATE DURING A WEDNESDAY VISITING DAY. Visitors came by car and rail from miles away to watch the mock, or sham, battles put on by the sailors, hear Lt. John Philip Sousa's band, and visit their sailors in training. Note the recruiting station tent near the gate. In *The Great Lakes Naval Training Station*, Francis Buzzell writes, "Imagine the scene that spread out before the visiting thousands on Wednesday afternoons during the summer of 1918. Imagine it! Forty-five thousand of the youth of the Middle West . . . swinging along to the martial music of America's greatest band; their white uniforms spotless, their rifles glinting in the sun, their faces bronzed and cheery."

NAVAL TANK. Station sailors built this with painted canvas over a wooden form.

LAND SHIPS USED IN SHAM BATTLES. Even on the grass of Ross Field, the U.S. Navy had ships.

SOUSA'S BAND AT GREAT LAKES. Lt. John Philip Sousa is in the first row, to the left of the drum major. The Great Lakes Band brought national attention to the training station. When the war started, the band numbered only 50 musicians. By the end of May 1917, it numbered 242. At peak strength, 1,500 musicians were organized into 14 regimental bands and a 300-piece band battalion. During the war, 3,056 musicians trained at Great Lakes. On special occasions, all 1,500 musicians would play on Ross Field. Several detachments of regimental bands traveled across the country to participate in Liberty Loan drives and other patriotic activities. The bands' activities went beyond fund-raising. Forty bands were sent aboard ship, and at the end of the war, Great Lakes sent 19 complete bands to play on returning troop transport ships.

THE GREAT LAKES REVUE. The Great Lakes Revue was a musical production to raise money for the Navy Relief Society. It played to sold-out audiences in Chicago and Waukegan. Musical numbers written by Jimmy O'Keefe, U.S. Navy, included "Good Bye America," "I've Been Waiting for You," and "When the Great Lakes Band Goes Marching on Parade."

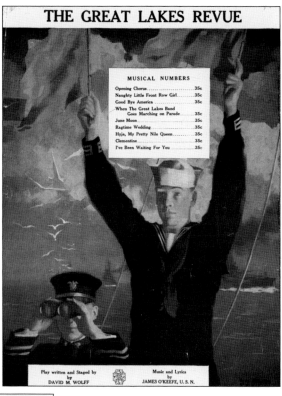

BENNY KUBELSKY. A local boy from Waukegan, Benny Kubelsky got involved in station theatrics and was a hit in the Great Lakes Revue. He would be known later in his professional life as Jack Benny, the comedian.

WORLD WAR I SHEET MUSIC. Behind a very youthful-looking Lt. John Philip Sousa are members of the Great Lakes Band and the administration building.

LT. JOHN PHILIP SOUSA. The driving force behind the tremendous success of the Great Lakes Band was, of course, the famous composer John Philip Sousa. Originally Capt. William Moffett invited Sousa to Great Lakes to discuss band matters and to recommend a bandmaster. Sousa volunteered to be the bandmaster and accepted a commission as a lieutenant in the Naval Reserve. Because Sousa had commitments with his private band, he asked for only $1 a month in pay. He twice turned down promotion to lieutenant commander, saying it "doesn't take a Lieutenant Commander to do this job."

"AFTERNOON RECREATION, A FRIENDLY BOUT." Athletic programs were also extremely important at Great Lakes. With the best coaching staffs in the country assembled by athletic director Comdr. John B. Kaufman, surgeon, U.S. Navy, Great Lakes manned teams in swimming, basketball, hockey, water polo, boxing, wrestling, and track and field. The station's store profits bought 10,000 bleacher seats, 396 football uniforms, 24,000 baseballs, 350 baseball uniforms, and 400 sets of boxing gloves.

FOOTBALL WIZARDS. The 1918 football team boasted an undefeated season playing against schools such as Iowa, Illinois, Purdue, Rutgers, and the Navy Midshipmen. The team brought together men who would go on to achieve renown in professional football, including George Halas and Jimmy Conzelman. The undefeated season concluded at the Rose Bowl, where Great Lakes defeated the Mare Island Marines 17-0.

YOUNG MEN WITH ENERGY TO BURN. The answer to extra energy was organized sports, from baseball, to tug-of-war, to track and field, to "cage ball," invented at Great Lakes. In addition to the high-profile Great Lakes varsity athletics, regimental competitions in baseball and football flourished throughout the war years.

WORLD WAR I—VIVE LA FRANCE. Great Lakes Naval Training Station recruits are seen here saluting the World War I French allies.

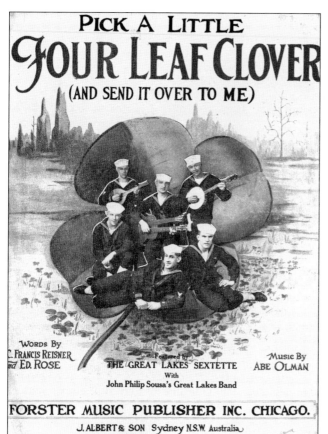

"PICK A LITTLE FOUR LEAF CLOVER," WORLD WAR I. This was a favorite song of the Great Lakes Sextette with Lt. John Philip Sousa's Great Lakes Band.

ARMS INSPECTION, 1917. A chief petty officer corrects a sailor's stance during rifle inspection. Temporary tent housing is seen in the background.

CAMP TENTS. Camp Paul Jones is seen here around 1917 from the administration building. The Navy Relief Society, Building 55, is under construction in the foreground. The background shows the hundreds of tents erected on a plot of land immediately north of the main station. The public works building has yet to be constructed on the vacant plot of land immediately east of Building 55 and west of Quarters J, which is barely visible at the far right of the photograph. (Courtesy of the Illinois State Historical Library.)

MORE TENTS. Tents are seen on Ross Field with the administration building and Brick Row in the background.

GRADUATES. One of the many graduating companies during World War I, Company I, 3rd

MOTOR TRANSPORT. Pictured here is the staff of the Motor Transportation Section of the Public

Regiment, is seen in October 1918.

Works Department on November 17, 1918.

Receiving Instructions in the use of the Compass,
U. S. Naval Training Station, Great Lakes, Ill.

DRILL TRAINING. This photograph shows compass training inside the main drill hall, Building Four.

"Assembling a Hydroplane," United States Naval Training Station, Great Lakes, Ill.

ASSEMBLING HYDROPLANES. World War I aviation carpenters and aviation mechanics assemble a hydroplane on the beach in front of the seaplane hangar. The power plant chimney in the background spews black smoke from the burning coal used to heat the station.

"Bag Inspection," U. S. Naval Training Station, Great Lakes, Ill.

BAG INSPECTION. Some things never change. World War I recruits await the results of their seabag inspection. Visible overhead are the recruits' beds, hammocks lashed to the ceiling. They were lowered to shoulder height at night.

BRIGADE RETURNS. A recruit brigade returns from a hike. The main drill hall, Building Four, is to the left, and the original instruction building, Building Three, is to the right. Building Four is now used as a gymnasium, and Building Three is the headquarters of the Training Support Center (formerly Service Schools Command).

FINAL INSPECTION. Recruits outside Camp Barry buildings stand their final inspection before shipping out. Their bedding lies rolled in front of them.

TEACHING RECRUITS TO LASH UP HAMMOCK.

HAMMOCKS. The evening prayer of a gob went as follows: "Now I swing me up to sleep, I hope I do not miss my leap. If I should fall before I wake, I know exactly where I'll ache."

OUTDOOR BOXING.

OUTDOOR BOXING. The prewar Atlantic Fleet boxing champion, Chief Turret Capt. John (Jack) F. Kennedy was assigned to the station as a gunnery instructor. His additional duties included managing the station boxing program. Boxing was very popular throughout the U.S. Navy because it did not take a lot of equipment and any number could participate. This scene is in the scenic ravine at Great Lakes, a popular spot for sporting events, church services, and other gatherings. Seats were eventually built along the incline, which formed a natural amphitheater.

Four

THE YEARS BETWEEN
THE WARS

After the war, military spending was cut. Most of the temporary buildings were torn down. Between 1918 and 1927, the station shrank from 1,200 to 495 acres, with only 63 buildings, including 42 officers' and petty officers' quarters.

To prevent permanent decline, a local campaign was organized in 1922 by the Union League Club of Chicago, the Association of Commerce of Chicago, and the Chambers of Commerce of Waukegan and North Chicago. These organizations demanded that Congress restore the station to at least its prewar status. With the election of Pres. Warren G. Harding, Congress approved funding passed that allowed Great Lakes to reestablish recruit training for 1,500 sailors (the original design population), an arrangement that continued through 1932.

The prosperity of the Roaring Twenties sparked a building phase at Great Lakes and a modern harbor costing $1 million was completed. The station was the scene of general recruit training and one special school devoted to the instruction of aviation mechanics.

In 1932, Pres. Herbert Hoover decided to rotate one-third of the fleet into reserve status each year to save $50 million. By July 1, 1933, U.S. Navy recruiting stopped. In 1932, the naval training station's Aviation Mechanics School moved to Norfolk, Virginia. A Marine Corps detachment was left to guard the station.

The local community rallied and again called for the training center to be opened. Following a vigorous campaign, the station was reopened on July 29, 1935, two years after closing. By the late 1930s, Pres. Franklin Roosevelt was preparing the United States for war. The Selective Service Act of 1940 fixed the draft for the next 18 months, and President Roosevelt ordered the U.S. Navy to convoy ships to Iceland and to chase German U-boats. In June 1940, reacting to events in Europe, Congress authorized $4 billion for a two-ocean navy. By September 1939, recruit training was reduced to eight weeks to meet the demand for sailors in the fleet. On July 1, 1940, training was reduced further to six weeks. Class A service schools (the new name for special schools) opened in December 1940.

The station began to expand. In 1940, contracts were granted for 14 barracks, a new galley, cooks' quarters, and other buildings. The capacity of the station increased to 14,000.

On December 7, 1941, the Japanese attacked Pearl Harbor, Hawaii. The United States immediately declared war on Japan. Germany reciprocated by declaring war on the United States.

COMPANY G, 15TH REGIMENT, AVIATION, MAY 15, 1920. Recruit training was discontinued briefly in 1922, leaving only two small schools in operation, the Radio School with 400 men and the Aviation Mechanics School with 80 men.

SAILORS POSE FOR A GRADUATION PHOTOGRAPH. Most of the sailors in this *c.* 1926 photograph are in undress white uniforms except for the sailor in dress white next to the chief petty officer. Dress white uniform traditionally had a navy collar and cuffs with white piping.

REOPENING. Great Lakes Naval Training Station officially reopened on July 29, 1935.

REAR ADM. JOHN DOWNES. Rear Adm. John Downes reopened the station in 1935 and returned in World War II to again lead the base through a busy time. He is the only commander to serve twice as head of the station. When Rear Admiral Downes arrived, he found the station in "a deplorable condition." He stated that "grass, except on Ross Field, has remained uncut and all buildings except the Administration Building are in a sad state of disrepair." By the time Rear Admiral Downes left in December 1936, the station was operating smoothly with a staff of 1,200, and recruits were receiving 12 weeks of training.

REVIEW. Seen in this *c.* 1935 photograph, recruits pass-in-review.

HONOR GRADUATE. This recruit is congratulated by Rear Adm. John Downes during a 1930s graduation on Ross Field.

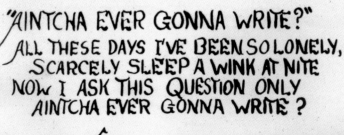

"AINTCHA EVER GONNA WRITE?"
ALL THESE DAYS I'VE BEEN SO LONELY,
  SCARCELY SLEEP A WINK AT NITE
NOW I ASK THIS QUESTION ONLY
  AINTCHA EVER GONNA WRITE?

EVERY HOUR I'VE BEEN WOND'RING
  I'M SO BLUE-CAN'T EAT A BITE
THEN THE MAILMAN PASSES THUND'RING
  AINTCHA EVER GONNA WRITE?

DO YOU REALLY MEAN TO PEEVE ME?
OR IS THERE SOMEONE ELSE IN SIGHT?
DON'T THINK THAT IT WILL GRIEVE ME
  HONEST, AINTCHA EVER GONNA WRITE?"

35

"AINTCHA EVER GONNA WRITE?" This 1930s postcard says it all.

U. S. NAVY POST CARD
A TIME SAVER FOR BUSY SAILORS
Use a Check Mark to Avoid Writer's Cramp and get more time to Eat and Sleep.

DEAR
- Sweetie
- Mother
- Dad
- Sister
- Friend
- Brother
- Shipmate

IT IS VERY
- Stormy
- Pleasant
- Hot
- Cold
- Unusual

I NEED
- Loving
- Money
- YOU
- Clothes
- Sleep

I SPEND MY SPARE TIME
- At Church
- In Bed
- Studying
- Working
- At Shows
- Thinking of You
- Eating

AND I AM
- Well
- Hungry
- Broke
- Lonesome
- Sleepy

MY WORK IS
- Enjoyable
- Tiresome
- Rotten
- Long
- Boring
- Insidious

AND I AM VERY
- Sorry
- Glad
- Thirsty
- Tight
- Sober

THE MEALS ARE
- Fierce
- Irregular
- Nourishing
- Poor
- Effective
- Worse

THANKS FOR THE
- Food
- Gin
- Tooth-paste
- Letter
- Clothes
- Money
- Listerine
- Advice
- Buggy-ride

Am having a wonderful time!

Wish you were here!

Regards to everyone!

YOURS
- Cordially
- With Love
- and YOURS only
- Always
- Respectfully

POSTCARD, 1930s. This postcard promises to be a "time saver for busy sailors" and instructs them to "Use a Check Mark to Avoid Writer's Cramp and get more time to Eat and Sleep."

HAMMOCK INSPECTION, C. 1935. Recruits present hammocks for inspection near the main-side barracks. Bedding had to be spotless, properly folded, and hammock lines coiled.

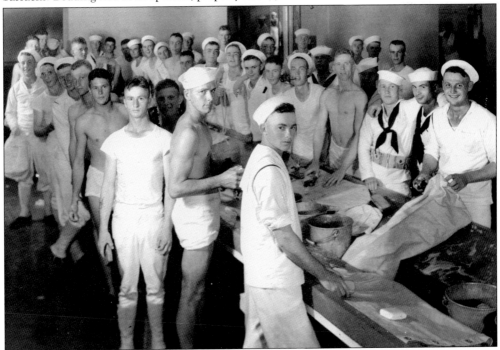

KI-YI BRUSHES AND SOAP FLAKES. Sailors, during the 1930s, scrub their seabags in the barracks laundry room.

Sailors at Chow. Pictured here is Building Five around 1935.

Formation in Main Drill Hall. Works Progress Administration (WPA) workers repaired the building and installed a white canvas ceiling covering in the 1930s.

RECRUITS LEARN TO SWIM. The original pool was in the basement of the main instruction building around 1935.

SEAMANSHIP INSTRUCTION, 1930S. Here is a group of Great Lakes recruits being instructed in proper seamanship. (Courtesy of the National Archives and Records Administration, Great Lakes Region. RG-181.)

PHYSICAL DRILL IN GYMNASIUM, 1930s. These recruits stand ready for their drills. (Courtesy of the National Archives and Records Administration, Great Lakes Region. RG-181.)

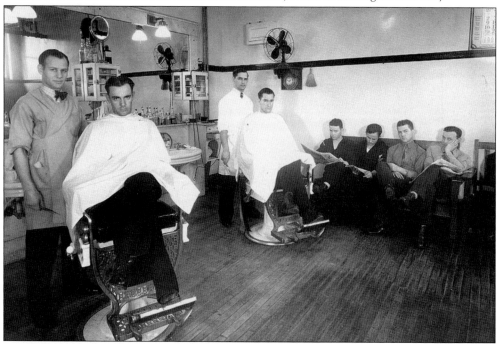

NEW RECRUITS RECEIVING FIRST HAIRCUT, 1930s. The first haircut has long been a rite of passage for new recruits. (Courtesy of the National Archives and Records Administration, Great Lakes Region. RG-181.)

MARKING FIRST ISSUES ON UNIFORMS, 1930S. Sailors learn the proper way to stencil their uniforms. (Courtesy of the National Archives and Records Administration, Great Lakes Region. RG-181.)

ROWING TEAM, 1930S. The inner harbor and boathouse are seen behind the sailors.

AERIAL VIEW OF THE BOATHOUSE AND INNER HARBOR. Some of the hospital buildings can be seen over the trees and left of the radio tower.

AERIAL VIEW OF CAMP BARRY, 1930S. The World War I hostess house can be seen to the north of the camp. The city of North Chicago is visible to the west, past the railroad tracks.

RECRUITS LEAVE FOR A HIKE FROM CAMP BARRY. The fence line to the left shows the original southern boundary of the base around 1935.

SHAM BATTLE ON ROSS FIELD, 1930s. Practice battles like the one pictured here are a critical part of preparing sailors for the real thing.

VISITORS WATCH A SHAM BATTLE, 1930s. Not only were the practice battles an important part of the training for sailors, they were a great spectator sport.

Airplane Hangars

AERIAL VIEW OF ROSS FIELD AND AREA TO THE NORTH, 1930s. The airplane hangars are shown north of the white athletic field house. The radio operators' quarters are visible below the towers. Ross Auditorium was not built until World War II.

AVIATION BEACH, GREAT LAKES, 1930s. Brick Row is visible on the bluff to the left.

NAVAL RESERVE SQUADRON, GREAT LAKES, 1933. This August 1933 photograph shows the

NAVAL SEAPLANE, GREAT LAKES, 1930s. Seaplanes like this one seem part of a bygone era, but they played an important role in the 1930s.

squadron posed in front of three of its airplanes.

AVIATION MECHANICS SCHOOL, 1930S. These students are learning the fine art of dealing with a propeller engine. (Courtesy of the National Archives and Records Administration, Great Lakes Region. RG-181)

. . . Great Lakes Bulletin . . .

U. S. S. BASS

U. S. Naval Training Station **Great Lakes, Illinois**

VOL. XII   Saturday, May 8, 1937   Number 1

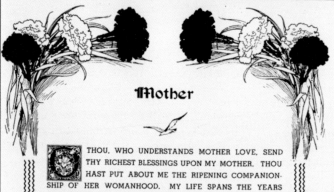

Mother

THOU, WHO UNDERSTANDS MOTHER LOVE, SEND THY RICHEST BLESSINGS UPON MY MOTHER. THOU HAST PUT ABOUT ME THE RIPENING COMPANION-SHIP OF HER WOMANHOOD. MY LIFE SPANS THE YEARS THAT HAVE CHANGED HER FROM YOUTH; MY EXPERIENCE HAS BEEN WON AT THE COST OF HER TOILINGS; MY FAILURES HAVE BROUGHT HER SECRET PAIN; MY FOOLISH PRIDE HAS MELTED BEFORE HER INDULGENT LOVE; MY MANHOOD HAS BEEN NURTURED BY HER CARE. ALL THAT IS HOLY IN ME COMES FROM HER UNSPOKEN TEACHINGS; ALL THAT IS WICKED HAS GATHERED OUT OF THE MOMENTS WHEN I HAD FORGOTTEN HER. GRANT UNTO HER IN THE APPROACHING DAYS WHEN HER GREAT LOVE WILL BE EMBODIED IN A FEEBLER FRAME, THE FRUITAGE OF HER YEARS OF LABOR. MAY THE LIFE OF HER SON BE FAIR FOR HER TO SEE. MAY PEACE BE THE COMPANION OF HER MEMORIES, AND CONFI-DENCE THE COMRADE OF HER MOTHER HOPES. MAY ALL THAT SHE ENDURED THAT I MIGHT BE FOR HER A JOY AND PRIDE BRING HER INTO A RICH HERITAGE. O FATHER, THOU HAST BEEN MERCIFUL THROUGH SUCH A MOTHER; MAY HER LIFE NEVER HAVE BEEN LIVED IN VAIN. AMEN.

E hope you will like the new masthead. To please our far-flung readers out on the West Coast who do not understand the greenery of local scenes, as well as to indoctrinate our local undergrads we thought it well to intersperse our graphic section with pictures of some of the war boats, the future homey cottages of most of us. There is much to be photographed hereabouts for the sake of our scrap book fiends, such,

(Continued On Page Four)

NAVY TALK

MOTHER'S DAY IN PEDRO

1000 - Revielle. The Mrs. turns on perco lator, grabs the cow extract off the stoop Looks out toward the sea and blesses th President or somebody for sending th Fleet to sea.

1030 - Finishes morning coffee and won ders what's the use in straightening u the house. Neighbor lady asks for bottle opener and leaves the Mrs. envying thes civilians who have husbands who neve go to sea or anyplace else without them Spotting practice my eye! Never has bee able to understand why the Fleet coul not turn the guns out toward Catalina an fire what they have to fire right at anchor That Spotting Practice reminds her t take that dress to the cleaners, the on that got chili all over it.

(Continued On Page Three)

BULLETIN. This May 8, 1937, *Great Lakes Bulletin* newspaper reminds sailors that the next day is Mother's Day. The *Great Lakes Bulletin* was first published in 1917 and is still published to this day.

Five

WORLD WAR II

Two hours after the Japanese strike at Pearl Harbor, the Great Lakes public works officer ordered construction of 32 barracks, two galleys, and other buildings on the north section of the station. Construction began the following day.

On December 7, 1941, there were 8,518 military personnel at the Great Lakes Naval Training Station. Six months later, with station capacity at 44,000, further expansion accommodated 24,000 additional men, bringing the capacity up to 68,000 in training. Late in September 1942, by replacing double-deck bunks for hammocks in all the barracks, the station increased the capacity to 100,000. The enlisted strength of the station peaked at 100,156 on March 19, 1944, more than doubling the World War I peak population. During World War II, a total of 965,259 recruits were trained at Great Lakes.

During this time, the number of recruits arriving at the station varied from 10,000 to 40,000 a month. This led to holdups in training and was offset by variations in the length of the training period. At the start of the war, recruit training had been set at six weeks. This period shortened rapidly to four weeks, then to three in an effort to accommodate an ever-increasing flow of recruits. At this point, arrangements were made to divert anticipated recruit overflow to Navy Pier, Chicago. In the first three months of 1942, several thousand recruits were sent to Navy Pier after receiving initial uniforms and equipment at Great Lakes.

Recruit training in the early months of World War II was loosely defined. In the three weeks a recruit was at boot camp, he received only a minimum of indoctrination along with his clothing, medical shots, selection tests, and service week. By January 1943, a full eight-week training program was in place. In all, the length of recruit training was adjusted 28 times during the war.

As part of an expanded aviation training program, two training aircraft carriers were used in Lake Michigan to teach carrier qualifications to student pilots. These became the USS *Wolverine* (IX-64) and the USS *Sable* (IX-81). These carriers anchored at Chicago's Municipal Pier, which quickly became known as Navy Pier.

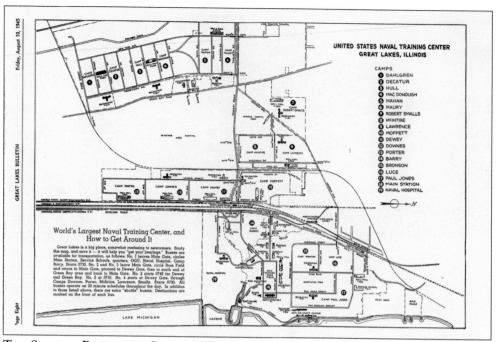

UNITED STATES NAVAL TRAINING CENTER
GREAT LAKES, ILLINOIS

CAMPS

1 DAHLGREN
2 DECATUR
3 HULL
4 MAC DONOUGH
5 MAHAN
6 MAURY
7 ROBERT SMALLS
8 McINTIRE
9 LAWRENCE
10 MOFFETT
11 DEWEY
12 DOWNES
13 PORTER
14 BARRY
15 BRONSON
16 LUCE
17 PAUL JONES
18 MAIN STATION
19 NAVAL HOSPITAL

World's Largest Naval Training Center, and
How to Get Around It

Great Lakes is a big place, somewhat confusing to newcomers. Study this map, and save it — it will help you "get your bearings." Busses are available for transportation, as follows: No. 1 leaves Main Gate, circles Main Station, Service Schools, quarters, OGU, Naval Hospital, Camp Barry. Starts 0730. No. 2 and No. 3 leave Main Gate, circle Ross Field and return to Main Gate, proceed to Dewey Gate, then to south end of Green Bay area and back to Main Gate. No. 2 starts 0740 for Dewey and Green Bay. No. 3 at 0730. No. 4 starts at Dewey Gate, through Camps Downes. Porter. McIntire. Lawrence. Smalls. Starts 0730. All busses operate on 20 minute schedules throughout the day. In addition to those listed above, there are extra "shuttle" busses. Destinations are marked on the front of each bus.

LAKE MICHIGAN   HARBOR

THE STATION BECOMES A CENTER. This 1944 map shows the base looking west (top) as it expanded out to Green Bay Road. No. 7 marks Camp Robert Smalls where the African American sailors were quartered.

LIFE AT NAVY PIER. This cartoon booklet shows a humorous side of radiomen training for men in the navy stationed at Navy Pier.

New Recruits. Whether Jackie, Gob, Mac, or Ricky, new recruits all take their first steps through the gates of the training center.

Personal Stuff. These World War II recruits carry their seabags and hammock bundles.

SEABAG LAYOUT POSTCARD.
Every recruit prepared his seabag
just like this for inspection.

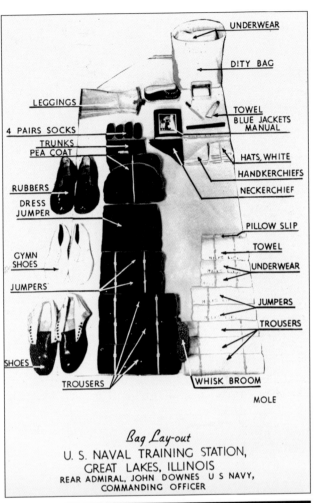

UNDERWEAR

DITY BAG

TOWEL
BLUE JACKETS
MANUAL

LEGGINGS

4 PAIRS SOCKS

TRUNKS
PEA COAT

HATS, WHITE

HANDKERCHIEFS

NECKERCHIEF

RUBBERS

DRESS
JUMPER

PILLOW SLIP

TOWEL

UNDERWEAR

GYMN
SHOES

JUMPERS

JUMPERS

TROUSERS

SHOES

WHISK BROOM

MOLE

TROUSERS

Bag Lay-out
U. S. NAVAL TRAINING STATION,
GREAT LAKES, ILLINOIS
REAR ADMIRAL, JOHN DOWNES U S NAVY,
COMMANDING OFFICER

SAILORS POSE WITH HAMMOCKS. Hammocks in the new camps were much lower than those in
World War I but were phased out by the end of the war.

WORLD WAR II RECRUIT STUDIES MANUAL. *The Bluejackets' Manual* could also be called "Everything You Ever Wanted to Know about Being a Sailor." The centennial edition was published in 2002 and is still issued to all recruits.

COMPANY 67, FEBRUARY 16, 1942. Nearly a million recruits would have their graduation photographs taken before the war was over.

GUNNERY INSTRUCTION. The duration of training was not the only aspect of boot camp that changed during the war. Training curriculum also changed. Chemical warfare instruction was added, swimming instruction was extended, seamanship tests were introduced with interregimental competition, the use of the Navy Standard Physical Fitness Test for each recruit was adopted, and enemy recognition training was added in August 1943. By 1944, training included more boat handling, firefighting, antiaircraft, radio material, basic engineering, special advance radio, cooks and bakers, and chief commissary stewards training.

SIGNPOST OUTSIDE THE OUT GOING UNIT. Sailors were sent to the Out Going Unit when their training was finished but before they were shipped out.

"MAC" LIMBERS UP

"'Mac' Limbers Up." Sailors were strengthened and kept fit through a variety of exercises, including football, baseball, tug-of-war, obstacle courses, swimming, wrestling, and boxing.

U. S. NAVAL TRAINING STATION, GREAT LAKES, ILLINOIS
REAR ADMIRAL JOHN DOWNES, U. S. NAVY, COMMANDING OFFICER

Anchored to Democracy. One of the special formations in World War II was designed after the popularity of those in World War I.

AMERICA'S SECURITY. Pictured here is another special formation.

U. S. NAVAL TRAINING STATION,
GREAT LAKES, ILLINOIS
REAR ADMIRAL, JOHN DOWNES U S NAVY,
COMMANDING OFFICER

WAVES' SECOND ANNIVERSARY CEREMONIES ON ROSS FIELD. In World War II, a women's auxiliary group nicknamed Women Accepted for Voluntary Emergency Service (WAVES) was established to release men for service in other areas of World War II. At first, its jobs were mostly clerical, but that would soon change.

WAVES DRUM AND BUGLE CORPS.

WAVES DRUM AND BUGLE CORPS AT GREAT LAKES. Women were not issued metal bugles but green plastic bugles. WAVES were first assigned to Great Lakes on November 10, 1942. The number increased rapidly and reached 658 enlisted and more than 100 officers in January 1943. As World War II progressed, they handled the U.S. Navy's mail, manned communications networks, and became instructors in chemical warfare techniques, aviation gunnery, instrument flying, and parachute rigging.

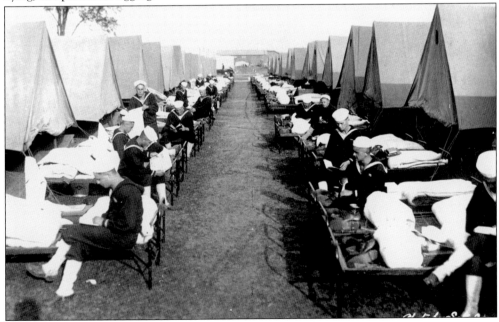

SAILORS OUTSIDE TENTS, WORLD WAR I. This image features some company quiet time. (Photograph by Chief Yeoman Sato.)

"FOR THIS WE FIGHT." Patriotic African Americans were frustrated by the early refusal to allow them to serve in combat ratings. In the early months of the war, the U.S. Navy department designated Great Lakes as the only site for training African American recruits. On June 5, 1942, the first African American recruit, Doreston Luke Carmen Jr., reported aboard. Within three months, "Negro service schools" had been established.

PRACTICAL RADIO THEORY. Many of the African American recruits chose more technical ratings such as radioman and learned tactical signaling and radio theory.

THE BLUEJACKET CHOIR ALBUM. It was the Bluejacket Choir that became famous for its Sunday radio broadcasts from Ross Theater. Chaplain Hjalmar Hanson organized this choir in the early part of December 1941. Because singers were constantly being sent to sea upon completion of their training at Great Lakes, the choir had a rapid turnover primarily. By the end of the war, 25,000 young men sang in the Bluejacket Choir.

CHOIR PATCH. Sailors in the Bluejacket Choir wore this patch on their sleeve.

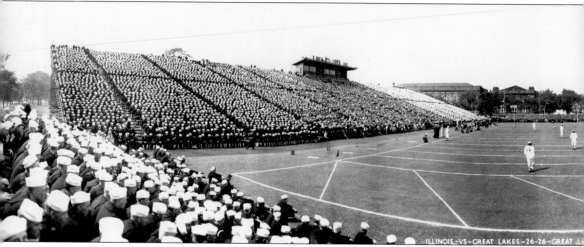

VIEW OF ROSS STADIUM, 1944. "We in the Navy definitely believe in the type of physical exercise and sports which involves bodily contact with your opponent," stated Secretary of the Navy Frank Knox. "This is a war where you kill or get killed! And I don't know anything that

WORLD WAR II FIREFIGHTING TRAINING. Good facilities were constructed for firefighting training, including four simulated carrier hangar decks, six open oil tanks, and six "Christmas

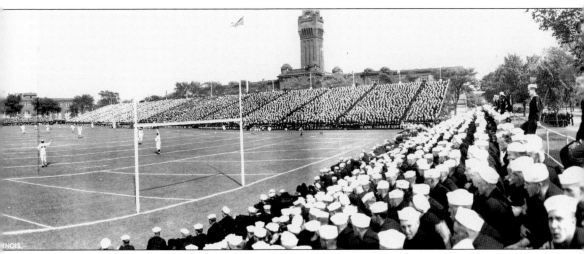

better prepares a man for bodily contact, including war, than the kind of training we get on a football field." This was printed in the *Great Lakes Bulletin* on February 11, 1944.

trees" which simulated ruptured gasoline lines. Actual shipboard firefighting equipment was used and about 720 recruits were trained daily.

HERE COMES THE NAVY

Souvenir Football Program

GREAT LAKES vs UNIVERSITY OF NOTRE DAME

SOLDIER FIELD, CHICAGO • *Price 25c* • **DECEMBER 5th, 1942**

GREAT LAKES FOOTBALL PROGRAM. The 1942 football team did not win any Rose Bowl championships, but it did win the 1943 award as the nation's top military team. It beat a previously undefeated Notre Dame team and played against Purdue, Northwestern, Iowa, Pittsburgh, Ohio State, Marquette, Indiana, and Western Michigan. Great Lakes played so well that an investigation was conducted to make sure that sailor-players were not being kept longer than necessary. Great Lakes was cleared.

THE LOG

PUBLISHED · **WEEKLY**

NAVAL · TRAINING
SCHOOL
NAVY PIER · ★✪★ · CHICAGO, ILL.

| Volume 1 | September 25, 1942 | Number 29 |

COMPETITIVE SWIMMING SCHEDULE ANNOUNCED

A swimming program designed as one of the most extensive ever undertaken in the service or out of it is being announced this week by the Navy Pier Athletic department, authorized by Lieut. (jg) J. D. Murphy and directed by G.C. Murphy, chief specialist. The program is devised to meet the yearnings of the advanced swimmers to enter competitive action, and at the same time serve as a morale builder to supplement similar setups which the Navy sanctions for reaching the greatest possible number of men.

In short, the undertaking is in the form of a tournament that will extend over a period of six months, beginning in October and winding up in March. The schedule is based on rivalry between the North and South Piers, and the outstanding team will be appropriately (continued on page10)

BOXING TOURNEY OPENS EARLY IN OCTOBER!

The completion of the new gymnasium and drill hall was all the Navy Pier Athletic department needed to touch off an explosion of plans for sports activity. The latest announcement ties in with the well-grounded claim that ours is the "fightingest" navy in the world. It reveals plans for a Navy Pier Golden Gloves tournament, winners of which will compete in the Chicago Tribune tournament later in the winter.

The meet will begin October 5th, and is open to all sailors and marines at the Pier, with the exception of those with professional experience. All weight classes will be included.

The list of awards covers a broad range, and it will by no means be necessary to win the championship in a certain class to get a prize. Every fighter who reaches (continued on page 6)

NAVAL TRAINING SCHOOL, NAVY PIER, CHICAGO, NEWSPAPER. The *Log* from September 25, 1942, appears here. The Naval Training School and Naval Air Technical Training Center were both wartime expansions of the schools at Great Lakes.

HOSTESS HOUSE – MAIN SIDE – BLDG. 42
U.S. NAVAL TRAINING STATION
GREAT LAKES, ILLINOIS

HOSTESS HOUSE INTERIOR. This very modern-looking building was designed by Gordon Bunshaft and built in 1942. It remains today as one of the few remaining examples of his early work. The building was used as a hostess house in World War II and was a relaxing place for sailors to meet friends, family, and sweethearts. Dance parties were also held for junior sailors who were too young to go off base.

WORLD WAR I RIFLE RANGE MEN. Men of Company J, 2nd Regiment, U.S. Naval Rifle Range (Camp Logan) are seen in this photograph.

RECRUIT CHOIR. The Bluejacket Choir poses in front of the instruction building in October 1941.

ORIGINAL BRICK BARRACKS. Pictured here are two of the original main-side barracks. These were used as supplemental classrooms in World War II.

BUGLERS. Shown here is the Service Schools Command Drum and Bugle Corps in September 1944.

BREEZE. The *Breeze* was the Naval Air Technical Training Center, Chicago, newspaper. Pictured is the November 30, 1944, issue.

SEGREGATED GUNNER'S MATE SCHOOL, WORLD WAR II. Before the war, minorities were limited to the steward rating. After the war started, the general ratings were opened to African American sailors. Camp Robert Smalls had its own shore patrol.

Tactical Signals

RADIOMAN SCHOOL
GREAT LAKES, ILLINOIS

TACTICAL SIGNALS. Even though the students were African American, the instructors were not. It would not be until these young sailors became more experienced that they would be able to fill instructor billets. Even athletic teams were segregated at the time, although one African American sailor, Marion Motley, did play on the varsity football team. African American officers were also trained at Great Lakes. In March 1944, 13 African American sailors graduated as the first black commissioned officers, 12 ensigns and one warrant officer. One of these "Golden Thirteen," as the group was called, went on to become a judge on the Illinois Appellate Court. Justice William S. White said, "We were the hopes and aspirations of the blacks in the Navy. We were the forerunners. What we did or did not do determined whether the program expanded or failed." Today the recruit in-processing building is dedicated to the Golden Thirteen and its contribution to history.

COACH. Lt. Paul Brown, who later coached the Cleveland Browns and who helped integrate football, was the Great Lakes football coach in 1944.

Boys in Hammocks
U. S. NAVAL TRAINING STATION, GREAT LAKES, ILLINOIS
REAR ADMIRAL, JOHN DOWNES U.S. NAVY, COMMANDING OFFICER

BOYS IN HAMMOCKS. Eventually sailors got the hang of sleeping in hammocks.

CARRIER OPERATIONS. As commander of the Ninth Naval District in World War II, Rear Adm. John Downes was ultimately responsible for naval operations throughout the Midwest. This included carrier qualification training on the USS *Wolverine* and USS *Sable* training aircraft carriers on Lake Michigan.

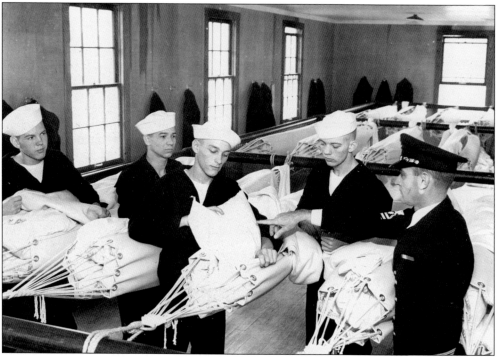

LEARNING TO MAKE UP HAMMOCKS. The U.S. naval training center in Great Lakes is seen around World War II.

MESS HALL. One could take all he wanted but had to "eat all you take."

NAVY SING. Even if a sailor was not good enough for the choir, everyone could follow Chief John Carter in a Navy Sing.

Orders to Move On
U.S. NAVAL TRAINING STATION, GREAT LAKES, ILLINOIS

ORDERS TO MOVE ON. World War II sailors still left by train. Their seabags are probably already stowed, but they carry their ditty bags with toiletries.

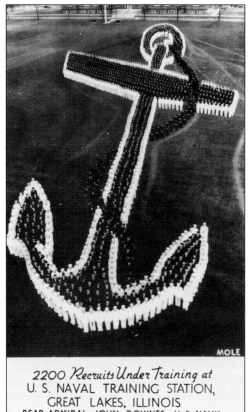

MOLE

2200 Recruits Under Training at
U. S. NAVAL TRAINING STATION,
GREAT LAKES, ILLINOIS
REAR ADMIRAL, JOHN DOWNES U S NAVY,
COMMANDING OFFICER

LIVING ANCHOR. Sometimes a recruit can point himself out in these pictures.

Six

AFTER THE WAR TO THE 1960s

With the end of the war, a call resounded to "bring our boys back home." The huge wartime military force was demobilized in record time.

The Great Lakes Naval Training Center was a critical part of this transition with the establishment of a separation center at Great Lakes on August 27, 1945. By December 14, 1945, it was announced that a record of 27,118 had been processed in one week. The separation center at Toledo, Ohio, was moved to Great Lakes in March 1946, further adding to the training center's responsibilities. The two-millionth sailor was released to inactive duty on March 29, 1946. By this time, two-thirds of the military demobilization had been completed. A year after it opened at Great Lakes, the separation center closed after releasing 450,000 U.S. Navy and Marine Corps men, women, and officers to inactive duty.

In the years following World War II, Great Lakes continued to train recruits, but recruit population levels varied greatly. At one point, there were so few recruits that various camps were closed to consolidate training facilities. In February 1946, the recruit training curriculum adapted to fit the changing times. Boot camp was reduced from 10 to 9 weeks.

In February 1950, a training program for reservists was instituted at Great Lakes. The U.S. Naval Reserve population during the fall, winter, and spring months averaged approximately 175 men per month, about half of what was expected. During the summer months, the number increased to about 3,500 men per month. A nine-week training program was instituted for some 300 to 500 reserve recruits per year. In 1958, a total of 546 recruits graduated from the nine-week course, while 9,297 reserve recruits received two weeks' training.

The Korean conflict in June 1950 demanded a rapid expansion of recruit training. Reservists were recalled to active duty and supplemented the Recruit Training Command staff. In 1951, the *Great Lakes Bulletin* reported, "In one seven-day period of the present emergency more men were ushered into recruit training than in any like period during World War II." A total of 68,943 recruits were trained at Great Lakes in 1951.

Two events occurred in 1957 that made recruit training a permanent part of the Great Lakes Naval Training Center. Naval Training Center, Bainbridge, Maryland, closed and a new construction program in Camps Dewey, Downes, and Porter at Recruit Training Command began.

THE GREAT LAKES PERSONNEL SEPARATION CENTER. "We know you're eager to get your discharge and start on your way home, and we are eager to help you get there quickly," says a caption on this map. After the war, the sailors and marines hailing from all over the Midwest were sent to Great Lakes Separation Center for discharge.

NUMBERS DISCHARGED. The sign reads, "This Dept. Has Discharged 34,396 Men to date."

IN-PROCESSING. New recruits in the 1950s report to Camp Barry for "in-processing."

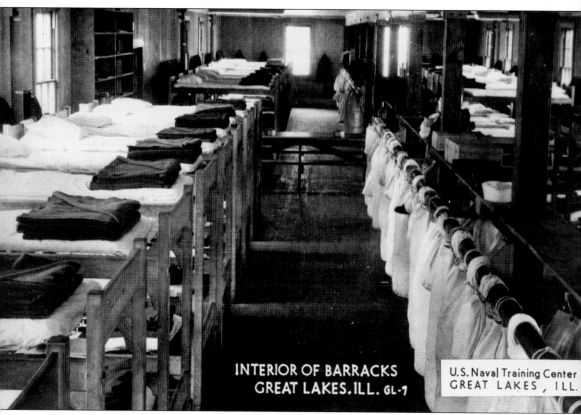

INTERIOR OF BARRACKS
GREAT LAKES.ILL. GL-7

U.S. Naval Training Center
GREAT LAKES, ILL.

VIEW OF OLD BARRACKS, 1950S. In 1957, ground was broken for a multimillion-dollar construction program at Recruit Training Command. When building was finished in 1965, Camp Barry was no longer used for Recruit Training Command headquarters or in-processing. Camps Porter, Downes, and Dewey included new barracks for two 5,000-man camps, with new galleys, classroom buildings, ship's company barracks, and dispensary. Administrative and in-processing activities, plus a 2,500-man camp, were consolidated in Camp Moffett.

***U.S. Naval Training Bulletin,
1948.*** "She's in the regular navy
now!" After passage of the Women's
Armed Services Integration Act in
1948, the first recruit training school
for women of the regular navy was
established at Great Lakes. Some
320 female recruits occupied the
two barracks assigned to them in
Camp Paul Jones. Women's training
expanded and continued at Great
Lakes until November 30, 1951, when
it was transferred to Naval Training
Center, Bainbridge, Maryland.

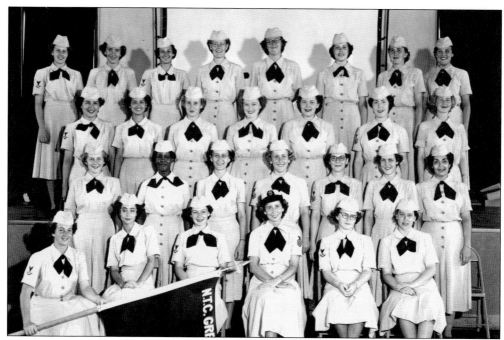

RECRUIT TRAINING (WOMEN) COMPANY 16, PLATOON 2. The women are wearing summer gray seersucker uniforms.

NINTH NAVAL DISTRICT

The News Letter
and NAVAL RESERVE BULLETIN

NO. 23 — 48   GREAT LAKES, ILLINOIS   MONDAY, 7 JUNE, 1948

DES MOINES, IOWA, RESERVE UNITS INCLUDE FIRST WAVE DIVISION IN UNITED STATES

READY ONE! Reserve gun crew at the Naval Training Center, Des Moines, Iowa drill on five inch 38 caliber loading machine in preparation for summer cruises and possible shipboard duties.

DES MOINES RESERVE UNITS INCLUDE CB'S, WAVES

Des Moines, Iowa, Organized Surface Battalion 9-14, was activated 1 August 1946 under the leadership of Cdr. C. H. Morgan, USNR, Inspector-Instructor, and LCdr. Theodore F. Grefe, USNR, Commanding Officer. Des Moines has achieved 90.8% of its authorized personnel allowance and has in operation three organized surface divisions — 9-54, Lt. A. D. Roberts commanding; 9-55, Lt. K. J. Dawson commanding; and 9-56, Lt. D. S. Powers commanding, as well as an organized CB company, 9-7, Lt. Clair C. Weintz commanding, and an organized CSA group, 9-19, with CSHCL Clarence S. Granquist in charge, all members of the Naval Reserve.

To Des Moines goes the distinction of activating the first volunteer WAVE unit in the United States, 9-1 (W), with Lt. Iris C. Anderson, USNR, in charge. As provided in recent directives, Des Moines WAVES have been assigned in limited numbers to serve with the organized reserve units in a volunteer drill pay status.

Des Moines also has a volunteer EW company, 9-33, under the direction of LCdr. John W. Albert, USNR and a NTS company, 9-17 (S), with LCdr. Robert D. Mullin, USNR, in charge.

The training center at Des Moines is favorably located in the business district of the city. It has one of the finest machine shop and diesel shop installations in the 9ND. Des Moines is the alternate control radio station for the western group of stations.

Enlisted men attached to the Naval Reserve in Des Moines may receive training as gunners mates, radiomen, electronics technicians, radarmen, machinist mates, motor machinist mates, electricians, boilermen, yeomen, storekeepers or hospital corpsmen.

During the flood emergency at Ottumwa, Iowa, in the summer of 1947, they were highly commended by the Commandant for their assistance to stranded residents of the flooded area.

FIRST SCIENTIFIC SEMINAR FOR NAVAL RESERVE OFFICERS TO BE HELD JUNE 9-23 BY OFFICE OF NAVAL RESEARCH

A total of 100 specially qualified Naval Reserve officers will observe and study Naval research programs at first hand during the first scientific seminar ever conducted for Reservists by the Navy, from June 9 to 23, 1948 in Washington, D. C.

The seminar, sponsored by the Office of Naval Research, will feature lectures by outstanding scientists and engineers closely identified with the scientific, research and development activities of the Naval Establishment, and visits to various laboratories in the Washington, D. C. area.

A number of the Naval Reserve officers attending the seminar are presently working as civilians on Navy research projects in university and college laboratories throughout the country.

Lecturers will include Dr. Detlev Bronk, chairman of the National Research Council and chairman of the Naval Research Advisory Committee; Rear Admiral Lewis Straus, USNR, member of the Atomic Energy Commission; Dr. L. R. Hafstad, Executive Secretary, Research and Development Board; Dr. Jacinto Steinhardt, Director of Operations Evaluation Group, Office of the Chief of Naval

Operations; Dr. Clark Goodman, associate professor of physics, Massachusetts Institute of Technology; and Captain Donald L. Hibbard, USNR, former director of the Special Devices Center, Office of Naval Research.

The two-weeks' seminar program also calls for visits to the Naval Research Laboratory, the new Naval Ordnance Laboratory, White Oak, Maryland; the David Taylor Model Basin, Carderock, Maryland; the Applied Physics Laboratory, Silver Spring, Maryland; Naval Medical Research Institute, Bethesda, Maryland; the Engineering Experiment Station and the United States Naval Academy, Annapolis, Maryland.

RESERVISTS WIFE MAKES BRASSARDS

Mrs. Arthur J. Hanley, wife of A. J. Hanley, AOM2/c has been sewing a fine seam for Battalion 9-51, according to the Dayton USNTC "ALNAV". The bright new brassards that the MAA's and OD's are wearing there are the result of Mrs. Hanleys' nimble needle—and for free, too.

THE NEWS LETTER AND NAVAL RESERVE BULLETIN. This is a typical example of the newsletter put out by the navy for the Ninth Naval District that included Great Lakes.

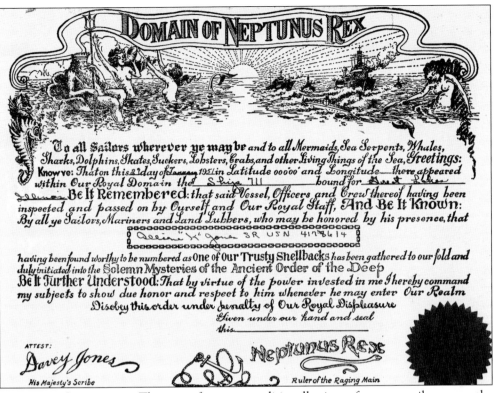

SHELLBACK CERTIFICATE. These certificates are traditionally given after a new sailor crosses the Equator for the first time, a rite of passage. This one belonged to Alliene Jones of Ship 711, Great Lakes, from January 2, 1951. It would be quite a while before women were routinely allowed to serve on real ships.

SEAMAN RECRUIT ALLIENE JONES AND SHIPMATES, 1950. Seaman recruit Alliene Jones and her shipmates are dressed for the cold weather in overcoats and havelocks over their garrison caps.

SEAMAN RECRUIT MINNIE WAUGH AND SHIPMATES, 1950. Minnie Waugh, second from right, is with her shipmates outside the women's barracks. She retired as a chief photographers' mate.

PERSONNEL INSPECTION, 1951. Seaman Waugh stands at personnel inspection at Great Lakes.

AT THE OARS. Recruits in small boat practice are seen on Lake Michigan around 1951. Recruits no longer train on the lake.

ROLLING CLOTHES. An old saying goes, "There's the right way, the wrong way and the Navy way!" Recruits learn the U.S. Navy way to roll their clothes.

WASH DAY. Recruits still washed their own clothes and hung them up to dry. If they were not hung just right, the chief would tear them down and have the whole company march over them.

SOFTBALL. This is a Great Lakes women's softball team around 1950.

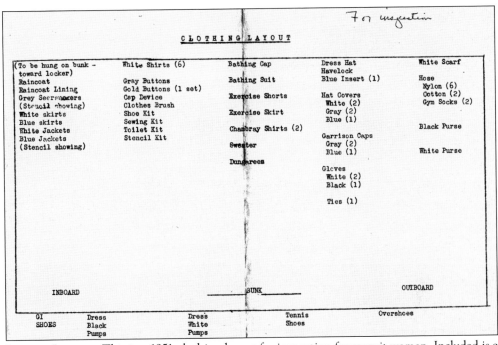

For inspection

C L O T H I N G   L A Y O U T

(To be hung on bunk – toward locker)	White Shirts (6)	Bathing Cap	Dress Hat	White Scarf
Raincoat	Gray Buttons	Bathing Suit	Havelock	Hose
Raincoat Lining	Gold Buttons (1 set)		Blue Insert (1)	Nylon (6)
Grey Seersuckers	Cap Device	Exercise Shorts		Cotton (2)
(Stencil showing)	Clothes Brush		Hat Covers	Gym Socks (2)
White skirts	Shoe Kit	Exercise Skirt	White (2)	
Blue skirts	Sewing Kit		Gray (2)	
White Jackets	Toilet Kit	Chambray Shirts (2)	Blue (1)	Black Purse
Blue Jackets	Stencil Kit			
(Stencil showing)		Sweater	Garrison Caps	
			Gray (2)	
		Dungarees	Blue (1)	White Purse
			Gloves	
			White (2)	
			Black (1)	
			Ties (1)	

INBOARD   BUNK   OUTBOARD

GI SHOES	Dress Black Pumps	Dress White Pumps	Tennis Shoes	Overshoes

LOCKER LAYOUT. This is a 1951 clothing layout for inspection for recruit women. Included is a bathing cap and suit, exercise skirt, cotton hose, and havelock. A havelock is a head covering that goes over the hat and is draped over the shoulders to keep out the rain.

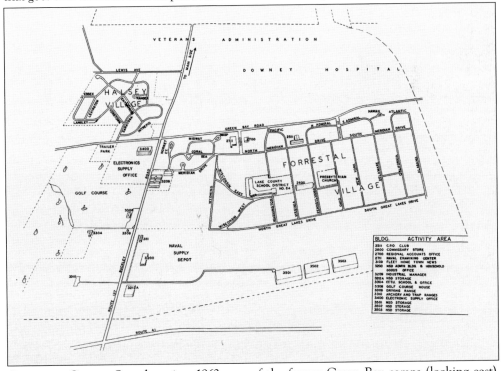

GREENBAY CAMPS. Seen here is a 1962 map of the former Green Bay camps (looking east). Halsey and Forrestal housing have been built, and the firefighting school is now a golf course.

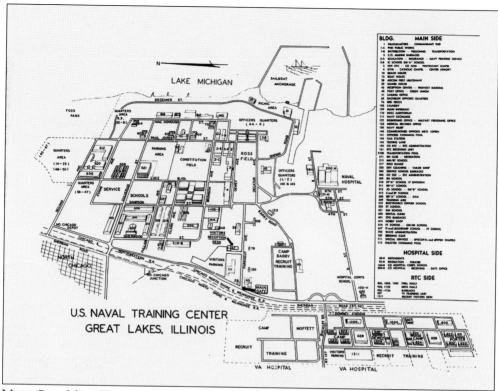

BLDG.	MAIN SIDE
1	HEADQUARTERS · COMMANDANT 9ND
1-A	9ND PUBLIC WORKS
1-B	DISTRIBUTION · PERSONNEL · TRANSPORTATION
2-A	C.O. MARINE BARRACKS
2-A	EDUCATION · INSURANCE · NAVY PRINTING SERVICE
3-A	SC SCHOOL BM "A" SCHOOL
5	CPO RTC · CO ADM · PROTESTANT CHAPEL
7	GYM · CATHOLIC CHAPEL · CENTER ARMORY
20	BOAT HOUSE
38	AEROM FIRST LIEUTENANT
39	GUARD HOUSE
42	RECEPTION CENTER · PROVOST MARSHAL
43	POST OFFICE · CREDIT UNION
51	SAILING OFFICE
63	BACHELOR OFFICERS QUARTERS
76	RED CROSS
105	LAUNDRY
109	MAIN INFIRMARY
110	ROSS AUDITORIUM
111	NAVY EXCHANGE
122	DISBURSING OFFICE · MILITARY PERSONNEL OFFICE
123	MEDICAL RECORDS OFFICE
130	NAVY RELIEF
140	COMMISSIONED OFFICERS MESS (OPEN)
141	OFFICERS SWIMMING POOL
142	TESTING LANE
150	CO RTC · RTC ADMINISTRATION
141	RTC RECEIVING UNIT
510B	TRANSPORTATION POOL
211	EM CLUB · RECREATION
213	MASTER SCHOOL
217	RIFLE RANGE
220	DRY CLEANING · TAILOR SHOP
300	SERVICE SCHOOLS BARRACKS
300	CO SSC · SSC ADMINISTRATION
309	DK SCHOOL
310	ET "A" SCHOOL · ET DIVISION
311	BM "A" SCHOOL
312	3O SCHOOL · BM "A" SCHOOL
412	E and EP SCHOOL
500	EM "A" SCHOOL · GYM
520	TRAINING AIDS
521	ELECTRONICS OFFICER SCHOOL
530	ET SCHOOL
531	BM SCHOOL
600	DENTAL CLINIC
601	CPO BARRACKS
614	HOBBY SHOP
676	FT SCHOOL · GM/M SCHOOL
677	IT and LEADERSHIP SCHOOL · FT SCHOOL
702	WAVE ADMINISTRATION
707	BEDDING ISSUE
711	SPECIAL SERVICES · EPISCOPAL and JEWISH CHAPELS
713	ENLISTED SWIMMING POOL

	HOSPITAL SIDE
28-H	DEPENDENTS
82-H	RECREATION · THEATER
100-H	CO HOSPITAL CORPS SCHOOL
200-H	CO HOSPITAL · RECEIVING · DUTY OFFICE

	RTC SIDE
800, 1000, 1200, 1300	DRILL HALLS
928, 1128	MESS HALLS
920—1126	BARRACKS
407	TV TRAINING UNIT
1311	RECRUIT VISITORS DESK

N

LAKE MICHIGAN

SAILBOAT ANCHORAGE

ZIEGEMIER ST.

PICNIC AREA

FOSS PARK

QUARTERS AREA

OFFICERS QUARTERS (AA - H)

MAC DONOUGH ST.

PAUL JONES ST.

PARKING AREA

CONSTITUTION FIELD

ROSS FIELD

QUARTERS AREA (14 - 25)

QUARTERS AREA (48 - 50)

LUCE BLVD.

QUARTERS AREA (36 - 47)

OFFICERS QUARTERS (L - 2) 142 & 143

200 M

NAVAL HOSPITAL

SERVICE

SCHOOLS

SAMPSON

NO. CHICAGO DEPOT

BIRKWOOD

CLARK ST.

FARRAGUT AVE.

VISITORS RECEPTION DESK

6TH ST.
5TH ST.
4TH ST.

SHERIDAN ROAD

NORTH CHICAGO

NORTHWESTERN R.R.

NO. CHICAGO JUNCTION

CHICAGO NORTH SHORE R.R.

CHICAGO NORTH SHORE & MILWAUKEE R.R.

VISITORS PARKING

MAIN GATE

CAMP BARRY RECRUIT TRAINING

HOSPITAL CORPS SCHOOL

U.S. NAVAL TRAINING CENTER
GREAT LAKES, ILLINOIS

SHERIDAN ROAD (RT. 42)

DOWNES STATION

CAMP MOFFETT

RECRUIT TRAINING

1311

VISITORS PARKING

VA HOSPITAL

VA HOSPITAL

CAMP PORTER

RECRUIT TRAINING

MAIN-SIDE MAP. Here is a 1962 map of the main side looking east. Recruit training areas include Camp Barry, Camp Moffett, and Camps Dewey, Downes, and Porter. These last three were later merged into Camp Porter.

CHROME DOMES. A recruit drum and bugle squad is seen in its "chrome domes" in this *c.* 1967 photograph.

LOCKERS. By 1969, the barracks have lockers—no more seabags hanging from the bunks.

INTO THE WATER. Recruits must all pass third-class swim qualifications. They are seen here around 1969.

BLUEJACKET CHOIR RECORD, 1960. Recorded music by the armed forces has always been popular with the public.

MORE BLUEJACKETS. Here is another 1960s Bluejacket Choir record.

STANDING INSPECTION. Old barracks were still in use in the early 1950s.

Seven

THE MODERN NAVY

By the early 1960s, Great Lakes was world's largest naval training center and a major center of technical schools, as well as the site of one of the U.S. Navy's largest hospitals and two large naval supply activities. The electronics supply office controlled the procurement and distribution of repair parts for the maintenance of electronic equipment at all naval activities. Ships throughout the world obtained equipment from the naval supply depot.

Great Lakes trained an average of 55,000 recruits each year and about 18,000 service schools students. Sailors received basic and advanced training as electronic technicians, machinists, gunners, hospital men, enginemen, fire control technicians (ordnance), radarmen, electricians, boiler men, journalists, optical men, instrument men, interior-communications specialists, and instructors.

Great Lakes was also the headquarters of the Ninth Naval District—the largest naval district in the nation, encompassing 13 midwestern states and directing the hundreds of naval activities, including the Naval Reserve program in the Midwest and its 120,000 reservists. These civilian-sailors received instruction in weekly drills at 72 training centers and also in annual cruises aboard ships and submarines of the Great Lakes training squadron. This squadron was affectionately known as the "Cornbelt Fleet."

The center moved into the 1970s with involvement in contemporary issues. Then chief of naval operation Adm. Elmo Zumwalt, famous for his "Z-gram" messages, wanted to make sure the U.S. Navy was fair and equitable in its policies and practices. He was very concerned with enlisted quality of life issues, racial tensions, and growing drug problems within the navy. All the center commands instituted a drug-awareness indoctrination program. The center also had a Committee on Equal Treatment and Opportunity (CETO), and each week the commander of the naval training center, with Service Schools Command, sponsored a seminar to promote racial understanding. Many of these practices continue today in varying forms. All U.S. Navy personnel are subject to random drug testing; ethic diversity is recognized and celebrated in formal ceremonies.

RECRUITING PAMPHLET, 1964.
Recruitment for training top-notch
seamen continued into the 1960s.

**SALT-AND-PEPPER SUMMER
UNIFORM.** The salt-and-pepper
summer uniform was practical, easy
to wear, and easy to keep clean.
The navy did away with it in the
mid-1980s.

MARCHING INTO DRILL HALL, GREAT LAKES, ILL. GL-16

U.S. Naval Training Center
GREAT LAKES, ILL.

DRILL HALL. Even with new construction, World War II drill halls like this remained in use. Drill Hall 1200, one of the last, was used for recruit graduations into the 21st century.

Welcome aboard...
the Navy's largest galley

Galley 928...

GREAT LAKES NAVAL TRAINING CENTER

THE NAVY'S LARGEST GALLEY.
Part of the new expansion in the 1960s was Galley 928 at Recruit Training Command.

BARRACKS INSPECTION. These sailors stand ready for inspection in this *c.* 1972 photograph.

BARRACKS STUDY, C. 1972. The life of a sailor is not all adventure on the open seas. Much of it is study in the classroom.

BEARDS. Along with salt-and-peppers, other uniform regulation changes allowed beards. When the order came to shave them in the 1980s, many weak chins reappeared. (U.S. Navy photograph.)

A CHANGE FROM JUMPERS. For a time in the late 1970s until the mid-1980s, the U.S. Navy tried out a new uniform for junior enlisted sailors. This "bus driver" uniform was the same as the officers and chiefs wore but with dull silver buttons. However, sailors wanted, and got back, their familiar cracker jacks. (U.S. Navy photograph.)

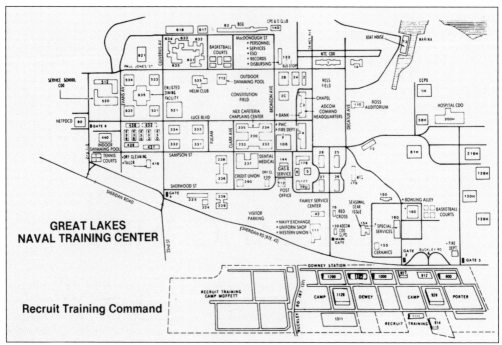

RECRUIT TRAINING COMMAND, C. 1982. This map shows the layout of the center in the early 1980s.

RECRUIT GRADUATION COMPANY. This c. 1980 photograph shows recruits at the culmination of the their studies and training.

Eight

BASE REALIGNMENT

More than once in its history, Great Lakes fought to remain a training center for the U.S. Navy. The Defense Base Realignment and Closure (BRAC) Commission decision of 1993 finally put an end to that fight and made Great Lakes Naval Training Center the navy's only and largest recruit training center. It also made Great Lakes the enlisted surface warfare training capital for the entire navy.

In 1992, the U.S. Navy had three recruit training facilities. The idea to consolidate recruit training and close two recruit training sites to save money threatened to once again close the training center at Great Lakes. Orlando, Florida, and San Diego, California, were the other two recruit training sites. Supporters of Recruit Training Command Orlando and San Diego argued their weather was better for training recruits. They would not have to find alternative ways to train during bad weather and would not have to use indoor facilities as extensively as Great Lakes. Considering the number of recruits that would go through training at a single-site recruit training command, building upkeep would be an important factor in any decision.

Base closure was a fiercely debated topic and there was much at stake. While most of the attention focused on the issue of a single-sited U.S. Navy boot camp, it was the service school facilities that tipped the scales in Great Lakes' favor. The biggest factors were the newly constructed "hot plant" propulsion trainers at Service Schools Command. Because moving and reconstructing these facilities would be exceedingly costly, the financial benefits of a single site at Great Lakes were evident.

After the decision to keep Great Lakes open, many changes were made. Recruit Training Command again trained woman recruits, returning women's training to where it originally started in 1948. The number of recruits trained each year at Great Lakes climbed from about 30,000 to over 53,000. Over 50 new courses would be moved to Great Lakes for A and C schools, almost doubling the number of students at Service Schools Command to 7,500. Many buildings that had been waiting for needed upkeep would finally be repaired.

The Blue Ribbon Panel focused on U.S. Navy requirements. As in the past, Great Lakes training was changed to meet real fleet requirements. Great Lakes Service Schools Command made changes of its own. Construction began on new living quarters and new or remodeled school buildings. Apprentice training moved from Recruit Training Command to Service Schools Command.

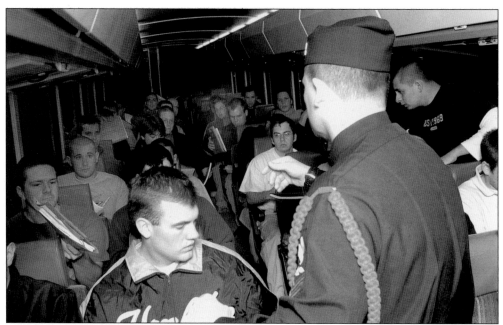

TRAVEL TO GREAT LAKES. Most of today's recruits fly into O'Hare International Airport in Chicago. There they meet at the USO and are brought by bus to Great Lakes. Until they have their "moment of truth," their last chance to confess to any lies on their applications, they still belong to navy recruiters. (U.S. Navy photograph.)

ATTEN-HUT! Recruits are seen in the Golden Thirteen. In the processing center, they receive their first lessons: how to stand at attention and the proper way to respond when a recruit division commander (RDC) asks a question. All recruits are formed into divisions of about 90 recruits and three RDCs man each division. RDCs are senior petty officers or chief petty officers specially chosen for their leadership and teaching abilities. They are identified by their red rope, or aiguillette, worn around their left shoulder. (U.S. Navy photograph.)

WOMEN RECRUITS AT UNIFORM ISSUE. Since BRAC, Recruit Training Command has been coed and recruits formed into brother/sister companies with half of the number men and half women. Roughly one-quarter of recruits are women. (U.S. Navy photograph.)

RECRUITS CALL HOME. Recruits get a quick telephone call home to let family know they have arrived safely. (U.S. Navy photograph.)

URINALYSIS. All recruits are drug tested within 24 hours of reporting aboard. The station has its own navy drug screening laboratory (NDSL) on base, and recruit results are back within hours. NDSL tests 560,000 samples a year, including those from the Training Support Center, U.S. Navy and Marine Corps Reserve centers, and recruiting districts, and from every military entrance processing station (MEPS) in the United States. (U.S. Navy photograph.)

RECRUITS IN FIREFIGHTING TRAINING. Learning to combat fires has remained as important a task as ever to recruits at Great Lakes. (U.S. Navy photograph.)

RECRUIT IN SCOTT AIR-PAK. All sailors must learn damage control and firefighting in order to protect their lives and their ships after accident or deliberate attack. (U.S. Navy photograph.)

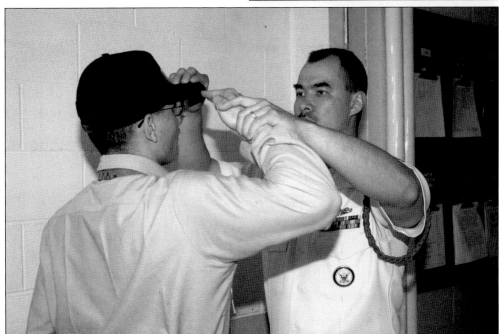

RDCs TEACH NAVY TRADITION, CUSTOMS, AND DISCIPLINE. During classroom and skills instruction, recruits learn how to adjust to and succeed within the U.S. Navy. (U.S. Navy photograph.)

SMALL ARMS TRAINING. A senior enlisted panel recommended more training in force protection, live-fire training with the Mossberg shotgun, and additional shooting of a 9-millimeter handgun. (U.S. Navy photograph.)

WATER SURVIVAL TRAINING. In addition to classroom training, recruits learn the fundaments of small arms marksmanship, seamanship, water survival, line handling, and firefighting. (U.S. Navy photograph.)

DRILL PRACTICE. During the first training week, divisions enter into competitive aspects of training. Excellence in academic achievement, military drill, cleanliness, and athletics all count toward earning recognition flags. Competition encourages teamwork and develops pride in achievement among recruits and among divisions. The climax of this competitive series is the pass-in-review practice where the best divisions earn Battle E, CNO (chief of naval operations), or hall of fame honors. (U.S. Navy photograph.)

COMBAT TRAINING POOL. Special training is also held here for special operations candidates. The attacks against the United States on Tuesday, September 11, 2001, brought rapid response at Great Lakes Naval Training Center. Increased security measures were immediately put in place, including concrete barriers and a shuttle service to move essential employees from remote parking lots to their work sites. The increased security did not affect the training of sailors in boot camp or those attending Service Schools Command and Hospital Corps School. Training in all three commands continued on schedule. (U.S. Navy photograph.)

JOSEPH WALLACE GREGG, FIRST GREAT LAKES RECRUIT. Joseph Wallace Gregg is buried in the station cemetery along with veterans from every war since World War I. (U.S. Navy photograph.)

THE LONE SAILOR STATUE. A symbol of the enlisted sailor, this statue stands in a park near the entrance of Recruit Training Command. The original statue stands at the United States Navy Memorial in Washington, D.C. The future of the U.S. Navy can be found in training at Great Lakes today. The young men and women who earn the right to be become sailors in today's navy will set the course for those who follow in the 21st century. They are the senior enlisted leaders and officers of the future, and their careers start here at Great Lakes. (U.S. Navy photograph.)

www.arcadiapublishing.com

Discover books about the town where you grew up, the cities where your friends and families live, the town where your parents met, or even that retirement spot you've been dreaming about. Our Web site provides history lovers with exclusive deals, advanced notification about new titles, e-mail alerts of author events, and much more.

Arcadia Publishing, the leading local history publisher in the United States, is committed to making history accessible and meaningful through publishing books that celebrate and preserve the heritage of America's people and places. Consistent with our mission to preserve history on a local level, this book was printed in South Carolina on American-made paper and manufactured entirely in the United States.

This book carries the accredited Forest Stewardship Council (FSC) label and is printed on 100 percent FSC-certified paper. Products carrying the FSC label are independently certified to assure consumers that they come from forests that are managed to meet the social, economic, and ecological needs of present and future generations.

FSC
Mixed Sources
Product group from well-managed forests and other controlled sources

Cert no. SW-COC-001530
www.fsc.org
© 1996 Forest Stewardship Council

Find Your Place in History.